Luke goes to a dude ranch.
He is a city dude.
Luke says, "I want to be a cowboy."

The dude ranch is huge.
Luke says, "There are many tall dunes.
I want to be a cowboy."

2

Luke pets a pony.
He feeds it a sugar cube.
Luke says, "I want to be a cowboy."

Luke sits on a mule.
He waves his hat.
Luke says, "I want to be a cowboy."

4

Luke feeds the sheep.
They are so cute.
Luke says, "I want to be a cowboy."

Luke uses a rope.
He makes a lasso.
Luke says, "I want to be a cowboy."

Luke sits by the fire.
He sings cowboy tunes.
Luke says, "I want to be a cowboy."

Luke is still a city dude.
But he will be back next June.
Luke says, "Now, I am a cowboy, too."

8